The 66 Laws of the Illuminati: The Secrets of Success
By The House of Illuminati

To contact the authors/The House of Illuminati, please write to:

The House of Illuminati
houseofilluminati@gmail.com

For Media and Investor Relations, contact
The House of Illuminati
houseofilluminati@gmail.com

Photo Credits:

Cover Photo: Ego Entertainment Productions, www.KingFamouz.com
Book Illustrations: Cameron Tyler

all those who enter into the House of Illuminati in search of the Light and its path to higher heights—Walk toward the Light and Success will come to you.

TABLE OF CONTENTS

INTRODUCTION

he 66 Laws of the Illuminati: Secrets of Success," written by The House of Illuminati, ovides the blueprint and tenets required for personal success. The House of Illuminati, own around the world as "The Illuminati," has broken years of silence with this blication. The Illuminati has made known its "Laws" which they indicate are the secrets success for anyone who embarks upon the path of Light.

Organized in six chapters, the book begins with "Chapter 1: The 66 Laws." Chapter 1 tails the sixty-six rules of life suggested by the Illuminati as a guaranteed guide to success. e Laws are age-old, proverbial wisdom which typically sheds light on a principle of good aracter. Each of the Laws is followed by a Lesson that gives further clarity; insight, eaning, and commentary to help the reader better understand how to apply the Law. apter 2, "A Letter to the Youth of the Present Age," is a letter written by the Illuminati to e youth of the 21st century. It is a passionate epistle in response to comments made by p artist Jay-Z and negative, inaccurate rumors which were circulating at the time. Chapter "The House of Illuminati," shares the ancient and modern history of Illuminati. Chapter 4, he Rituals," is a behind-the-scenes look at what happens inside the secret House including lmission criteria and ceremonies. Chapter 5, "The Creed," and Chapter 6, "The Prayer," blish the Illuminati's creed and prayer which shape the essence of what the Illuminati elieves.

For the first time in centuries, this book is the only known source of written ocuments which define The Illuminati. A detailed account of our purpose and our ommitment to the "path of Light" is provided for the public. The Illuminati hopes that all aders around the world will unite in a common cause to pursue the Light and travel down road of success. Success is guaranteed to any person who follows the Laws and learns om the Lessons.

n the path of the Light,

he Illuminati

CHAPTER 1

The Laws: The Secrets of Success

Chapter 1

The Laws of the House of Illuminati:
The Secrets of Success

These are the hidden Laws of the House of Illuminati, ancient in form and applicable in this present age. Learn the Laws and their Lessons according to the level of your Commitment. All those who do will be successful.

Law 1

There is a light within you that the world did not give to you. You must let the light within you shine!

Lesson 1: The spirit of the divine dwells within you. When your Creator made you and formed you in the womb, light was placed within you, your purpose was placed within you, your destiny was placed within you. Every person on Earth has a responsibility to make a significant contribution through the use of his or her talents and gifts. You must be true to the call of the genuine within you. Once you figure out your gift and train yourself for its use, then you must let it shine so that the world can see. If you are a painter, paint so well that all the masters say here lived the best painter on Earth. If you are a doctor, practice the healing arts so well that even those in the grave say that he was the best medicine-man alive. If you are a singer, sing so well that even the heavenly choir must give an ear. Your success depends on you having the courage to use your gifts! The Creator gave you the gifts to use.

Law 2

Show love to those who show love to you and take care of those

who have taken care of you.

Lesson 2: You have to show love to everyone. If you want the people to love you, you must also love the people. Show even more love to the people who have supported you along the way. Don't ever forget the people who were with you from the beginning. Thank your Creator and your parents for getting you here—love them with all your heart. Thank your teachers and your friends—always show them love for who would you be without them? Love the people and your success is guaranteed. Remember though, that where there is love, heartache is always near.

Law 3

Respect your haters—acknowledge them, thank them, and rise to higher heights. Love your haters, and wish good upon those who would do you wrong.

Lesson 3: The haters you always have with you. Some of them will be close to you and others will not even have met you a day in your life. You will be hated for doing both good and bad. Don't be worried when the haters speak against you. Sometimes their hate has nothing to do with you. There are people who don't want you to be successful and it has nothing to do with you as a person. Sometimes your success will remind many of their failures. They will resort to many acts of darkness to see you fail. But listen, when the haters speak, thank them for their words and opinions. They might actually be of benefit to you. No matter how petty their remarks may appear, keep the high road and rise to higher heights. Love your haters, show them love, and wish success upon them as well. Hate no one and always let your words be positive to those whom you do not know. Never speak negatively about anyone that you do not know. You can criticize, but do so in love.

Law 4

Make plans— write your dreams into reality.

Lesson 4: Your thoughts can become reality. Those with the light but without a plan are equal in stature to those with no light at all. The importance of a plan cannot be stressed enough in the execution of your purpose. It is paramount to your success and imperative to your contribution to this side of life because your years are limited. Habakkuk 2: states: "And the Lord answered me, and said, write the vision, and make it plain upon tablets, that he may run that readeth it." If we take the converse of this, it equates to: the one who does not write the vision, and the one who does not make it plain upon tablets does not progress because he has no goals to achieve. Though plans change often, their benefits are that they provide a guide to measure your success in obtaining your dreams.

Planning we do naturally. For example, when we need some items from the market, without much conscious thought, we determine which market to go to, how we shall arrive there—by foot or horse, and what path we should travel. We have the image in our minds exactly... all of this without needing to write any of it. Why? Because this, my friend, is something we have done time and time again. Something that we could probably do with our eyes covered. But to do something you have never done before like visiting one of our brothers at the Coliseum in Rome, requires a plan. The details of such a plan can be arduous. However, the more detailed the plan and the clearer the vision, the more likely the end-result will show itself. After all, the House of Illuminati did not create itself out of thin air. It came to be because of dedication to a plan.

Law 5

Always be a man or woman of your word.

esson 5: Keep this Law close to your heart. A man or woman is only as good as their ord. There are people who depend upon you to be true to what you say. If you say that ou will do something—do it! Or immediately let the person know that you are unable to o so. Contracts, bonds, and relationships will be made upon your word. Let your word e true and real. Others will judge your dependability based upon what you say that you ill do and what you actually do. If these two are ever far apart, you have cast yourself to a web of lies and deceit, where even your honesty will be questioned.

Law 6

If a compromise is required in order to save your family or the House, then consider it.

Lesson 6: Do not ever compromise yourself as a person. Don't do anything that i against your own moral code. There are many things that we say that we will never do i life. Sometimes, on rare occasions, there are some things that require compromise i order to save the family or the House. For example, the man of the house may find i necessary to say, "I'm sorry," or "I love you," in order to keep the family together. W often feel that we are right however we can be dead wrong. Some contracts will requir that there be some mutual benefit on both sides. You may have to give some concession to the other side so that you can gain more in the end. Use wisdom and apply the Laws i determining when compromising is best for the family.

Law 7

Pay your debts.

esson 7: Pay your debts. Pay your bills and pay them on time. Make arrangements to
y your bills should you not be able to pay what you owe. Your credit history and credit
orthiness are important. People will loan to you what they feel you can pay back. In
'e you will always have bills, just pay them. Your wealth is not determined by what you
ive but rather by what you can borrow. Only those seen as dependable will receive the
enefit of credit.

Law 8

Preserve life at all cost. Don't waste bullets.

Lesson 8: Fight only when necessary. Show force only when it is needed. You become weak when you always use your strength. Punishment does not mean death. Crush your enemy only if they will never accept peace. Never use a show of force unnecessarily and never show your weapons. There is only one time when you are justified to endanger the light and life of someone else and that is when the dark actions of someone else put your life and light within an inch of being no more. And even then, death should not be the aim. Love everyone to the point where you have nothing but respect for their life and presence on Earth. There are many ways to take your opponent out without the use of deadly force. Even more so, the use of a gun for reasons other than war is unmanly. In this regard, one should never bully another person.

Law 9

he House of Illuminati will only promote those who have studied

their craft and are prepared for the next level.

esson 9:   Life and successful progression in the light requires learning. Success quires knowledge. You must know the basics—reading, writing, and arithmetic—in der to be a good soldier of the light.   If you want to be a violinist, then you have to udy the scales of music. If you want to be a singer, then you have to sing. Being ccessful at your craft requires that you study. And how can you lead others if you have ot studied. Only those who have gained the knowledge will be promoted.

Law 10

The art of compromise should be skillfully employed so that you always keep the advantage.   Negotiate with your best interest in mind.

Lesson 10:   Compromising is a skill. The compromise must be negotiated to achieve or maintain the best advantage for you. If you must give something up, give up that which will cause the least amount of loss to the overall goal. It is wise not to put all of your chips on the table.

Law II

Guard your light and protect it from self-harm. Your body is a temple for the light.

Lesson 11: This fact: your body is a temple for the light—is very important. Take care of your body, it is your temple. Eat healthy and drink plenty of water. Do not smoke herbs that alter your mind and do not indulge too much in alcohol. You must protect your inner organs. Your brain is the gateway for which light creates. If you destroy your lungs, you also destroy your brain. And if you destroy your brain, your entire temple will fail. Only put things in the temple that will help to build it up. Do not eat or drink those things which will tear it down. Smoking is one of the worst acts that you can do to the temple. Be good to your temple, for you will only get one. The kinder you are too your body in your youth, the better it will be in your old age. Not only is your diet important but also seek to be as stress free as possible. Negative stress is a silent killer and it will destroy the light. Guard your temple which protects your light.

Law 12

Honor your mother and father for their light is a part of your light and their light brought you into the Light. You honor the Greater Light when you respect your parents.

Lesson 12: Respect your mother because you passed through her. Respect your father because his light mixed with your mother's light in getting you here. Honor them all of their days. They cared for you when you could not care for yourself. This too honors the Greater Light.

Before you begin the journey of discovering who you are, your purpose, and how you want to make a contribution, you must first understand that your light is a combination of two: the light of your mother and the light of your father. If for no other reason (even if they make no contribution to your success), they must be respected as your parents. By disrespecting them you are like a soldier using the dagger in his right hand to stab himself in his left arm. It hurts only you. By condemning them, you are diminishing who you are and thus dimming your light. In the House of Illuminati, we have discovered that the high-minded and mighty tend to regard themselves as self-made. This is foolishness. This behavior is not tolerated and will lead to your dismissal from the House. Once you leave there is no returning back. Therefore, show your parents as much love as possible.

Law 13

Know yourself and your enemies—learn both your ways and their ways. Discover your upper and lower limits

₃sson 13: One of the grandest miscalculations of man is to believe he has no enemies. ₃r he who has no enemies, apparently, is doing nothing, has nothing, and aspires to be ₃thing. At all cost, you should avoid the company of those who do not wish you well. ₃fortunately, this is not always possible. Therefore, minimal contact will suffice. In the ₃ent that you must be in the same room with your enemies, evaluate your tolerance of ₃eir snide comments, remarks and sometimes blatant disrespect. Disregard it. You ₃ould be well prepared in dealing with their ways already. You should also be even ₃ore aware of yourself and how well you handle these situations. Flight or fight instincts ₃pically surface, but fighting must always be a last resort. Choose to flee instead. The ₃atness of the earth provides you with much terrain and many places to find yourself. ₃lso, you should not preoccupy yourself with the possibility of gaining the friendship of ₃ese people either. Seldom will you get it, and if you do, be wary of it. A sage once gave ₃is parable of a young man in a dilemma. The young man had received a hat given to ₃m by his late father. He really liked this hat. But when he wore it his "friends" mocked ₃m. He came to the old sage and said, "If I wear it they will mock me, but if I don't wear ₃ I will feel like I have given into their mocking." The sage responded: "Well, it sounds ₃ me that if you wear it or if you don't you are doing it for them…" Take this lesson and ₃member exhausting yourself mentally about your enemy serves to your detriment. It ₃quires too much energy and too much time—energy you should be using for the light. ₃o this instead: act as if you do not see them, but know that they are there. Give them the ₃ame respect you would give anyone. But watch them, learn them, and study them.

Law 14

Know your strengths and your weaknesses—surround yourself

with those whose light compliments your weaknesses.

Lesson 14: It is good to know the things which you are strong at and the things that you are not good at. If you know the things that you have some degree of skill, you will know how much work you are able to do. When you know your weaknesses, you know the areas that you must devote more time and work. Get a tutor. Study in the areas that need more attention. Surround yourself with people who know more than you do in the areas that you are weak. You will need their strengths to assist you along your journey toward success. It only makes sense that if you don't know how to do something that you need someone on your team who does.

Law 15

There can only be one boss and their can only be one head of the

House.

esson 15: Respect the family and its structure—know your role and your place. Too any cooks will spoil the soup and too many managers will create chaos. Somewhere it as written that: "No one can serve two masters. Either you will hate the one and love e other, or you will be devoted to the one and despise the other. You cannot serve both od and money." Respect the boss and the leader of the House for your time will come.

Law 16

Know when to sign the contract and when to walk away.

Lesson 16: Do not accept every deal. Some deals are not for you. Sometimes the fine prin
will make what looks like a good deal turn out to be bad one in the long run. Sign the
contract only when the best terms are achieved for you and your concerns. If a good dea
cannot be achieved then walk away with no regrets. Keep working and stay on the path
Opportunity sometimes knocks only once but so does Death. Keep striving until the righ
door opens for you but do not sign the contract unless it is the best deal for you. Also keep
in mind that sometimes your word will bind you into a contract. Be specific about the
things that you say you will and can do.

Law 17

Remember that everything good is not always good for you.

Lesson 17: Use your Third Eye to discern the truth. Too much of anything can be bad for you. There will be some sweet deals that offer you the world, but it may not be good for you. Some matters require wisdom and keen insight—a sharp eye that looks beneath the surface. Be willing to cut a road where no one has traveled before. Refer back to Law 16.

Law 18

Don't sell or prostitute or your light. Don't lose your light or your

soul for fame and fortune.

Lesson 18: Your light, which is your divine gift, is not for sell. The Greatest Light has endowed you with a gift to share with the world to make it a better place, not to make profits and money. Making money is not an end; it's just a necessity to keep food on the table for your family. You can lose your soul while gaining the whole world when you lose sight of what's important. Stay true to the calling of the Light and your divine purpose. Don't sell out. And if you have to sell out, then it's not worth it and it surely will not last. You will eventually fail and your illusion of success will disappear. Success requires hard work. There is no easy way to the top. It takes longer to get to the top from the bottom, than it does to get to the bottom from the top. Slow and steady, just keep progressing and eventually you will make it. Fame and fortune is a trap. Celebrity status brings pain—just seek to be the best one on Earth at your craft. Losing your light ain't worth your soul. Climb the ladder of success with your dignity and integrity intact. To the rare few who think that it's okay to sleep their way to the top—success will not last. Save yourself the heartache and trouble. Don't let your ambition lead you places that your ability cannot follow. Arrive at the top on your own merits and success will be fruitful.

Law 19

What happens in the House of Illuminati, stays in the House of Illuminati. Keep the business of the light to yourself and only the brothers and sisters of the light.

Lesson 19: House business is only meant for those in the House. What goes on in the House, stays in the House. Don't share everything with everyone. Don't put all your business in the streets. Guard what is secret and protect that which is sacred. Be careful who you tell your business because everyone does not have your best interest in mind. Some things may be used against you at a later date. Be selective in what you share and think twice before you speak. Either find a trusted confidant or share with those who already know.

Law 20

Do not seek fame, but instead seek to let your light shine and

fame and fortune shall follow.

Lesson 20: Find a career that will take care of you and your family. You are your brother's keeper and your sister's keeper. Success, fame, and fortune will happen once you let your light shine.

Law 21

Never back a man into a corner unless you are prepared to fight,

for you will enter the fight of your life as well.

esson 21: "I have witnessed the most spiritually downtrodden man, the most lowly of a ul, the most feeble in character and in courage, a coward, fight with the vengeance of 0 of Alexander's best trained soldiers when fighting is his only option." When walls do t permit themselves to be jumped over or walked around, then one will go through em. This applies to the beasts of the field and even to the gods. Most importantly, it plies to humans. The reactions of men are at best an approximation in any rcumstance, but in this regard we are certain: a man backed into a corner, given no her option, will fight to the death. If you are the one backing him into a corner, then be epared to face the fight of your life. This applies to business, love, politics and religion. your goal is hostility, then face him—antagonize him. If your goal is diplomacy, then t beside him—be friendly toward him.

Law 22

Money, power, respect—of these three, respect is the most important; make sure that you always give respect regardless if the person is friend or foe. Self-respect is the greatest of the respects.

Lesson 22: What is money and power without self-respect? You can have money but you must respect yourself in the way in which it was gained. Power without respect usually turns into fear and disdain. People will either love you or fear you—rarely both at the same time. Don't worry about gaining the respect of persons, just do your craft and use your light so well that the world will give you respect. Give respect to everyone including your foe. When you lose respect for your opponent, you are likely to lose the battle, for you are apt to underestimate his ability. A small man with an ounce of self respect, the right skill, and strategy can topple a big man.

Law 23

Always be humble.

esson 23: Loving the people requires humility. If you are arrogant or place yourself ove the people you will lose touch and your support. Cockiness and confidence may crease your swag but they both must be utilized wisely and responsibly. Too much of e or the other is not healthy. Maintain the common touch and never let them see you ming. Only announce your presence when your only aim is to be seen. Too much ash and bling-bling is neither cute nor becoming of an expert. You must look the part t you must possess more substance than style. Style is always secondary to substance.

Law 24

Remember that the young shall one day be old. Be active. Prepar

in the days of your youth

for the days when you are old.

Lesson 24: Beloved, we want success now and quickly. But sometimes success won'
come in the days of your youth. So you have to prepare for it. You only live once bu
you could live a very long time. Y.O.L.O. does not give you a right to live recklessly an
destroy the temple in which the light dwells. Nor does it mean that you don't prepare fo
tomorrow. Longevity has its place; nonetheless, enjoy the days of your youth. The
energy of your youth is at an all time high especially for the young men—the strength o
your energy at 16 will not be there when you are 66. Be warned that arousal wil
decrease as your age increases. Guard your temple accordingly and keep it healthy
There is a saying that goes, "Youth is wasted on the young." To a degree this is true
Mature understanding usually comes after the days of youth. Be careful of the
foolishness that you take part in while you are young, because some of it my follow you
along the path. Don't waste all your money on things that don't even matter. And most
importantly, the more talents you learn in your younger days, the easier your older days
shall be.

Many men have died waiting to find their purpose. A lot of talent is buried in the
graveyard. One person may discover his purpose at age 5 and another at age 54. While
you are on the path to discovering your purpose, do not be complacent and wasteful of
your time and energy—neither of which can be returned to you. A scribe once wrote:
"We find ourselves in such predicaments where the young clamor about from one thing
to the next with no real focus or clear aim or commitment, or the old man who has
scripted his cause, determined his struggle and defined his contribution, yet he finds
himself with no energy to execute his magnificent plans….a pity, isn't it?" At the very
least, one must walk away from this Law knowing that regardless if you discover your
light or not, you must be active in this dash of a life between the year you are born and
the year you die. Certainly there have existed men who discovered their purpose on the
day they died and if they had not enjoyed life to that point, then may their regrets flee
from their souls like their souls fled from their corpses. Regret is often caused by
inactivity, and inactivity has befallen us all at some point. Still, one must fight against it.

mply stated: there are things I cannot do at 66 that I could do at 23. Better make use of ur youth. One day it will not be with you and the sooner you discover your purpose, e better off the world will be.

Law 25

Make offers that cannot be refused. Tell people what you want,

politely. He who asks is he who receives.

Lesson 25: When you make an offer, make it so good that no one will refuse it. Whe you want something, be polite when you ask for it. To demand something in a nasty wa will increase the chances that you won't get it and you will surely create an enemy. As nicely, and say, "Thank you."

The basic principle that the one who asks most often receives should be a principle s ingrained that it warrants no writing. Be direct and do not beat around the bush in askin for the things that you want. For example, the cry of a baby makes strangers eager t solve the baby's need. It makes us cringe to hear that call for help. It speaks to us Normally, it can be boiled down to the desire for food or to be comfortable. Though th baby can't even say specifically what it wants, mothers in particular will go to hell if th solution is there. Ask and you receive—you may not receive what you want but at leas you will get attention to your concern. The most important thing is that you know wha you want before you ask. Assess your needs and ask in the most polite way. Next yo need to figure who best to ask to provide an answer to your question. Determine this an the doors to the Enlightened One may one day be open unto you.

Law 26

Always be fair—be just and seek justice where justice is due.

Lesson 26: Be fair and treat all persons equally. Don't ever knowingly cheat anyone out of anything for which you know they are due. Be just in all your actions and seek justice when you know a wrong has been committed. Silence is never an option. When you are silent, you are just as guilty as the one who did wrong. Fairness builds respect. And where there is respect, there is power.

Law 27

Take care of your children and teach your children in the ways of the light and encourage them to be the best at whatever talent has been gifted them.

Lesson 27: The Children of the Light are the most important beings on Earth. If you have children, take care of them. Do not abandon them when they need you most. As parents, you don't have to love one another but you do have to love your children. Children should be the greatest priority. If you have them, encourage them to strengthen their talents and learn as much as they can. Take them to school—insist that they are educated in the sciences, maths, language arts, social studies, athletics, music, and the arts. Protect and educate them at all costs!

There is nothing more despicable than a father who is well versed in the arts, English, French, arithmetic, and the Bible, but has children who cannot distinguish between their right and left hands...children that cannot read and write. There is nothing worse than a mother who in her intellect knows that it is good to keep herself in good shape and posture, but leaves her daughter to wear rags. Whether you are a workingman or aristocracy, educate your children.

The light finds itself either used or unused—there is no in between. Parents are either positioning their children for success by encouraging and supporting them or positioning their children for failure by discouraging their light and killing their inner spirit. Children are best engineered to work toward the light within the realm of two parents. In the traditions of society, yes, mother and father are ideal. In the traditions of the Illuminati, we respect and appreciate alternative love and living scenarios equally. We accept it and love it. It is more common than the masses think. Children who reside in families with 2 fathers or 2 mothers; or in the care of grandparents; or of only 1 parent can be just as successful as any other child. If they are equipped to succeed and encouraged outwardly, they will grow a spirit of dauntlessness that will make them immovable in the sight of unfairness and unstoppable in the face of injustice. They will maximize their light because of their initial struggle. Be sure to guide them in the light and surely they will follow. And if they follow, they will surely succeed.

Law 28

Make things right when you have committed a wrong.

Lesson 28: This one is simple. If you have done something wrong, then make it right Restore any loss that you have created. Don't be afraid to say, "I'm sorry," if you know the fault is yours. Accidents happen, but if it's your fault, then take responsibility. Taking responsibility for one's action is tantamount to being successful and a good leader.

Law 29

Observe much, speak less, and learn more. Listen more than you speak—we have two ears and one mouth for a reason!

Lesson 29: Few are masterful in the art of speaking. For those who are articulate, find it be a real asset. To be skilled in the art of speaking, you must be well practiced. For the majority of those who find themselves on the other side of the spectrum, it would be wiser to observe much, speak less, and learn more. Proverbs states: *Even a fool is counted wise when he is silent.* Think of the most foolish person that you know and certainly it is because of what he or she says. He talks too much—a blabbermouth—and often without substance. If you do find yourself speaking, you should be succinct in your questions and responses, and upfront about your knowledge or lack thereof. Being silent when you are unsure does not undermine you, but being loud and wrong does. You should never lay all your cards on the table anyway. A wise man will always listen more than he speaks. Learn to listen well and success will surely follow.

Law 30

Don't put everything on the table—save some just in case.

Lesson 30: Always play the game of life smartly—use your common sense. Keep the advantage in your corner. If you tell your opponents everything, then they will have the advantage. They will know all of what you know and all of what they know.

Law 31

If it's too good to be true, then more than likely it's too good to be

true.

Lesson 31: Beloved, if the deal seems too good to be true, just assume that it is. Read the fine print. Ask questions until you feel comfortable. No one can offer you the world without hard work and dedication on your part. No one can offer you the world anyway because no one owns it. Be a skeptic and use your Third Eye.

Law 32

You always have two options: peace or war. If you have to choose, always choose peace. War leads to destruction of the light and to the family. If you must enter war, do so with the clear aim of achieving peace.

Lesson 32: Peace is always better than war. When at peace, the Light can create freely. When at peace, the mind has the ability to think. When at peace, the temple can operate effectively. War causes destruction to yourself and the ones you love. You must love peace more than you hate your enemy—hate is an act of darkness. No family has ever benefited from prolonged war. Families function best in peace. If one decides to use their light and energy for war, the goal of doing so must be to get your enemy to submit to peace. Peace should prevail and war should be entered as the very last option.

Law 33

Revenge will destroy the light and weaken the family. Revenge should always be avoided but if it comes down to it, then revenge must be balanced with justice. But in the House of Illuminati, the only revenge is success!

Lesson 33: Revenge dampens your light because it causes you to focus on things which make no contribution to your success. Repay a wrong with kindness. Show love to your enemies and it will eat them up. Love is the only revenge that you need. Illuminati is not concerned with revenge, only success. Be just in all your actions. Although ancient leaders warned that if you leave your enemy standing, he will return to destroy you. Illuminati does not support such actions. Always use the light and wisdom to avoid war and revenge. Matter of fact, the only true revenge is for you to succeed in your goals. When an enemy wants you to fail, then the most long-lasting revenge is for you to rise to higher heights, prevail against the odds, and achieve success in whatever your goals! Stick it to your enemy by being successful. Imagine the sting when you achieve in spite of all odds.

Law 34

Continued success requires continued improvement. Some things must be earned with a slow determination—too much too soon can be deadly. Captains must earn their rank.

Lesson 34: In order to reach higher heights and climb the ladder of success, you have to work hard. You have to study along the way to keep the mind and light fresh. You have to practice your gifts so that you can get better at them. Practice makes you better. Continued education is a requirement in order for you to remain fresh in your craft. Hard work is a given and success is earned. If it is handed to you, you will not last long. If you give a person too much power too soon, it will consume him. You have to be trained first before you can hold power effectively. No one would let a baby run the house—some things will come with time. If you want to lead, first learn what it is like to be a follower.

Law 35

First and foremost, acknowledge God, the creator of the Light—in all things that you do. God is the supreme leader of the children of the light.

Lesson 35: Seek first the Greatest Light and ask that wisdom be added unto you. Give credit to the Greatest Light for allowing you to exist on Earth and for giving your inner light. Your talents are gifts from God, don't waste them and do not abuse them. Thank God for all that you are able to do.

Law 36

When shit gets real, stay calm. Remain calm in all situations

Lesson 36: Never let them see you stress. Remain calm in all situations. Do not appear to be shook over the little things. Stay calm and work it out.

Law 37

Your life must mean something; otherwise your living will be in

vain.

esson 37: Seek to be great. You become great by making a significant contribution in e lives of others in the world. If you chose to do nothing with your life, then your ving is in vain and you have wasted your light. Everyone has the ability to do mething to help someone else along the way. Everyone has a purpose. Join forces if ou need to but do something good with your life—at the very least, help someone.

Law 38

Be watchful of the time, for there are limited hours of light in a day. Always be on time to your appointed place.

Lesson 38: Illuminati always wear watches—read the Rituals to know what the officia watch of the Illuminati looks like. You should never leave the house without a watch Illuminati are always mindful of the time. Illuminati are not late to meetings and wil always send a message should they be delayed. Divide and plan your day according t the hours of light. A good night's sleep is helpful for the day. However there are time where we must forego sleep in order to the get the work done.

There will certainly come a day where daylight will be accessible 24 hours. Men will on day work late into the night because he has discovered how to produce a wax-less candle one that can burn with more utility, one that can light more space and area, one that car ultimately allow him to work longer. The downside to this is that man will become mor inefficient. He will sleep more and later and he will procrastinate more because he knows that with this new candle he can "work" later into the night. We must remain watchful o the time because perception of time will change, but time itself will not. Sunlight is the true dictate of time, not some invention of man. Nonetheless we will find ourselves seduced by this notion of more light, which in turn means more work, which in turn means more productivity, which affords more resources—this is wrong.

Law 39

Don't be afraid to go the desert road alone. Travel lightly.

Lesson 39: Sometimes you have to travel alone (Acts 8:13-40). Do not be afraid to set out on the path of your light and success alone. Sometimes you have to leave home in order to seek success. And along the way, you will discover many things about yourself. Be independent and self-sufficient but do not be afraid to ask for help if needed. There is a reason the milk from your mother's breast only lasts for a limited period. Travel lightly—walk toward the light and with as little emotional and physical baggage as possible.

Law 40

Keep your appearance decent in public at all times.

Lesson 40: "Come as you are"—a belief of the church, but does not apply to th members of the House of the Illuminati. We do not accept that. The most obvious sig that a person is, or is not, a member of the House, is his clothing. Clothing that is il fitting, too big or too small, is distasteful. Only those dressed appropriately will ever b considered into the House. However, we do recognize the need for costumes per se in th execution of your purpose. For if your purpose is to be a clown, then by all means whe performing your clown duties, wear your clown gear. Yet, one should never be seen i such a manner on a regular day. To his children, he would be an embarrassment. Equally it is an embarrassment to have a mother who dresses herself in the manner of a prostitute for the daughter learns that this is acceptable, and the son endures the mocking of hi friends because of his mother's inappropriate appearance. Because of your understandin of your light, your love of yourself, and most importantly the respect of the House, yo will dress appropriately. This Law is as old as the House but stays current with th present time. Accept it, respect it, and appreciate it because it will bring yo understanding, love, and respect in the eyes of the public—of which we are the leaders.

Law 41

ake care of your own house before you take care of the house of others—make your bed in the morning.

esson 41: How can you go out to contribute to a world, yet you cannot find the time to ganize where you lay your head at night? It is inconsistent that one claims to be a pillar the community when his house is not in order. Since our beginnings, we have scovered that all great minds are consistent in one thing: making their beds. If they did t do it themselves, they had someone else do it, but they refused to enter a bed that was tidy, and unprepared to receive them. One of the intellects put it best: "I never lay in a oppy bed because kings and queens certainly don't....only pigs do." This has informed r belief that how you do one thing is how you do everything. Making your bed is an portant component in getting your day started correctly. It shows the soul that "I" am portant and "I" am worthy. It slows the mind in rushing off to start the day. It tells the iverse that sparing five minutes to prepare my resting place will not cripple my ability complete my goals for today. Most importantly, be responsible for your actions.

Law 42

Don't precede your spoken words with "Let me be honest" or

"Real talk".

Lesson 42: A man should never betray himself in his own speech. This can be no mor
evident than when you begin your statements with the phrases: "Let me be honest" c
"real talk." Never should you trust what is said after these statements. And everythin_
said before them should be looked upon with a microscope of discernment. Never us_
them because it gives the impression that what you have spoken before the words wer_
uttered was either not true, only partially true, or you were not confident in you_
perspective. This is considered a form of hedging, but perhaps this would be bette_
termed a form of hiding. Consider this: instead of "Let me be honest," insert th_
statement "let me not lie," and now instead of "real talk," insert the statement "false tall_
aside." They are equal. Would you believe anyone that used them? Therefore you shoul_
rid your speech of them because "real talk" makes you sound unreal. And "let me b_
honest" makes you sound like a liar.

Law 43

You should never make assumptions.

esson 43: The House of Illuminati will never be misguided by assumptions. Great ouses have fallen because of this, so we take this Law from their misfortune. Our aim is e mark. Missing it is unacceptable. Contrition is forbidden. We are clear, upfront, and rect. If the wisest of men measures 10 times and cuts once, we measure 11 times cause we are the wisest of the wise. All interactions of man, the fall of great kingdoms, e demise of individuals, the end of great warriors, have come because of assumptions. hose who assume, early and often, become sloppy and do so because they have chosen live in fantasy rather than fact. Remember this: we never get what we expect, but what e inspect. A great philosopher once said: "To assume is to make an Ass out of U and le." Members, for us, to assume will rock the foundation, bend our supports and shake ar roof, which can lead to the destruction of the House. The body of the House is only as rong as its supports.

Law 44

Give your time to those things which are important.

Lesson 44: I cannot be mined, packaged, stored or saved. I am not a solid, a gas nor am a liquid. Yet I can be both described qualitatively and quantitatively. What am I? I am time. The most basic of economic principles states that resources are scarce. Knowing this, one should be careful to manage them. Time is a resource. But a resource like no other. This is a resource that cannot be replenished, that is why it should be guarded like the virginity of your only daughter. You must keep watch of it. You must protect your time from being stolen from you. You must know what you are spending most of your time doing, and consider if it is building toward your light or the light of the House. If it is not, then you are wasting your time. You must determine what is most important to you, and what is most important in developing the House. If you had to choose between being robbed of your most precious jewel or your time, your time is more precious than the most precious of stones. It is on par with the value of life. Both should be preserved at all costs. Because your time is so precious, you should only give attention to that which builds you, not what tears you down. People want to steal it, so do not let them. The latest gossips of the day, the rumors about you or another, and the news of nonsense all serve to do one thing: distract you. So be aware. If you are taking garbage in constantly, then you will only get garbage out. If you only take the latest gossip in then you will only get gossip out. It will seep through your pores like you have a diet of raw garlic causing you to reek. Remember you are what you eat. You become what you spend your time doing. Make time for the things which are important to you.

Law 45

In order to get the work done, you must show up.

Lesson 45: Simply be where you are to be when you are supposed to be there. Show up. This is simple, basic, and obvious. Yet this separates us from the average. Showing up does not require considerable thought. It is merely an action taken. Do it. There is more to gain from being present than you can gain from being absent. Because if you fail to show up, there is a person you could miss meeting, a piece of information you can miss learning, or an opportunity you can miss seeing. These opportunities rarely present themselves again. If you must be late, make no excuses but always be considerate to anyone who may be waiting on you. The man who is on time is in a better position than the one who is late, but the one who does not show up is in no position at all.

Law 46

Learn how to live with rejection. Rejection is not always defeat.

Lesson 46: Members of the House, those who flee at the sight of the possibility c rejection are those who have decided that living a defeated life is more comfortable tha living a life where success and opportunity are possible. There was a story that told of beautiful princess who wed the ugliest man in the land. She later was asked, "Young fa. princess who could have had any man here or far, why have you chosen him?" Sh responded, "He was the only man who asked." Others had gawked at her beauty, stared a her ways, dreamt about being with her one day while none of them simply asked. The were too afraid, and unwilling to risk rejection. Because of his willingness to face th possibility of rejection, he won her affection, her respect and her admiration. Because o his willingness to lose, this time he won. Do not forget that those who swallow the pill o rejection are dangerous. For they have determined that what you think of them is n longer important. What is important is the opportunity and the mission to accomplish it— nothing else. Often times, attaining the goal is not as important as going to bed wit either rejection or regret. One of them eats at you like a poisonous vine, while the othe allows you to sleep in peace knowing that "at least I gave it a try." The Council mus warn that sometimes a "No" means "No." For example, should a woman refuse a mar and tell him, "No," then "No," means "No." Do not proceed further, just accept the "No' and go to sleep.

Law 47

Learn to say "Okay" convincingly—it is not the most important thing to win an argument...sometimes you gain more in defeat.

Lesson 47: "Okay" is one of the most delightful words to speak. It does not necessarily mean yes or no, yet it frees you from the burden of the issue in question. An okay can stop an argument, allowing the parties involved to relax and comeback to revisit the issue later. It must be noted that in the House one must not fret over trivial wins like children do. House members must realize that sometimes you gain more in defeat than you do in victory. For the war is the most important accomplishment, not the battle. Sun Tzu said: "The Supreme art of war is to subdue the enemy without fighting." If we are to remain strong for the future, we must right these words upon our hearts and forget them not, for they will be promising to us if followed, or lead to our demise if ignored.

Law 48

Shake hands, look people in the eye. You can tell a lot about a

man from his grip.

Lesson 48: Learn the Illuminati Grip in the Rituals. A handshake lets a person know who you are. When you do the Illuminati grip, conceal with your left hand the right hand grip. Whenever you shake hands, look the other person in the eye. A handshake seals the deal.

Law 49

You should know your craft like the back of your hand.

┃sson: 49: You must know your craft better than the back of your hand. It is
┃acceptable not to. It is your gift, your light, and your contribution to the world.
┃cause it is your craft, it is important that you not only know your craft, you must
┃derstand the history of it, its major players, and you must know how to position
┃urself to be the best at it. If you are a master swordsman, you must be able to converse
┃out swordsmanship like it is art; you must converse about it like Michelangelo would
┃scribe the art he did for the Sistine Chapel. It allows the other person to enter your
┃orld and see into it. It helps you articulate your vision, dreams, and your purpose.
┃ithout this, you are letting the House down. To say "I am just a soldier," disrespects the
┃ntributions that great warriors like Genghis Khan, Alexander the Great, Napolean, Sun
┃zu and others have made. You must know these men like they are your brothers.
┃ssentially they are. Though you may not share common blood, personal belief, or even
┃nes, you do share one thing: a spirit laden with undying passion in perfecting the art of
┃ar. By knowing these men when difficulty comes you are able to summon their spirits
┃r guidance. By knowing the history of your craft, you are able to truly believe in it. And
┃y doing these two you position yourself to become the most skilled. One day, the
┃udent shall become the teacher. So it follows, that one day greats shall become gods.
┃he House only accepts those that strive to walk amongst the gods.

Law 50

Remain selfless in serving others.

Lesson 50: Sit back and see creation—you will become inspired. The creations of the Heavens, as well as of man are magnificent when you realize these were once a thought We must, at all times, seek to create and fulfill our need to create for others. I have see man work at the speed of 10 horses when he knows that his family, friends, an community are dependent upon his good works. This must be understood that the person who creates for himself does a good thing, but the one who creates for others sleeps with a full belly—he ensures that his children's children will do so as well. If you are descendent of the most high who created the Heavens, Earth, the animals, trees, bugs man and so on, then you should be able to contribute something, correct? Remember by holding the thought of your progeny and the friends and family of today, you can double your efforts and geometrically increase your results in building for the future.

Law 51

Make excellence a habit. After the team finishes its grind, you must continue grinding.

esson 51: You will be a part of a team in pursuit of excellence. Seldom will you reach our full potential alone. Therefore you will encounter various personalities with various bilities but all looking to accomplish one thing: success. Everyone one wants to live osperously in the light. In order for you to illuminate to your highest degree you must o more than your team. You must in your own gift practice and perfect it as best you an. If you, as a group member, are seen as the best spokesman, then it is not enough for ou to merely improve your speech as the group does. You must also in your own time y yourself, practice, practice, and practice. You must do so even if that means just one ore minute, one more word. These sorts of repetitions add up and grow your abilities nmensely. The Enlightened One came to be because he spent extra time reviewing his udies, perfecting his craft, studying the laws of the House, and the perspectives of Men. xcellence is a habit. It must be cultivated, watered and weeded before it can fully ossom. It must be practiced daily.

Law 52

Rise early in the morning and work late into the night but divide your time for family, work, and love accordingly.

Lesson 52: African Proverb: "Every morning in Africa, a gazelle wakes up. It knows it must run faster than the fastest lion or it will be killed. Every morning a lion wakes up. I knows it must outrun the slowest gazelle or it will starve to death. It does not matter it you are a lion or a gazelle. When the sun comes up, you better start running." We in the House of the Illuminati are not permitted to sleep like the others. We because of our possession of the light have the responsibility to work and produce in the hours where the Lord himself may agree are unholy. Yet, we must rise early to get the work done. We must do this because our friends and family require our time as well. It is not wise to neglect them. To build a great House, we must strive to neglect as little as possible—this includes work and family. Remember, time is more precious than any other resource therefore, we must be tactful in our use of it. There will be times you will have to forego sleep because you must work or attend to the needs of your family. There will be times when you forget to eat because you will be so engrossed in the moment at hand. That is why it is important to sleep when you are supposed to. Though the day will be extended by the inventions of man, he is at best when he is on schedule with the sun. Keep to this routine because you are far more efficient and effective living a life in line with the rise and set of the sun. You are far more successful in hunting in the day than you are in the night; and likewise you are a far more elusive and difficult to catch in the night than the day.

Law 53

Never be afraid to try and never be afraid to fail. Go do it, start now, and make it happen and if you fail, "So what!"

Lesson 53: The truth of the matter is you will always be afraid to try and to fail. We are wired with this fear. Still you must not allow this fear to cripple you. You must understand how it manifests in your mind and body, and you must counteract it. You must beat it. Here is some wisdom about fear and prehistoric man that will help you manage your fear. There were once two brothers attempting to capture a boar. All that separated them from the boar was a lake. The first brother, fearless, jumped into the lake and swam to the other side while the other hesitated and just looked on, never diving into the water. Once the first brother arose at the edge of the lake on the other side, he glared back in disgust at his brother for his cowardice. The second brother stared at his brother terrified at what he saw creeping up behind. Immediately as the first brother turned back around to capture the boar, a crocodile snapped him in two dragging his torso back into the lake. Though the second brother did not eat that day, he lived to recount the death of his brother who feared nothing. We are descendants of the second brother, born perceptive of danger and wired to fear. The difference is that we rarely encounter dangers like our ancestors, yet we still interpret fear the same way. We have taken a real fear— loss of life for example—and altered it into a fear of being told "no" by someone we want to court or a fear of a project becoming a fruitless waste of time, instead of something evolutionary. We have turned this fear of death into "what will they think about me?" The best opposition to these sorts of fears is to take action immediately. Pursue your objective while the mind is as clear as the sky before the doubts creep in like grey clouds threatening to rain on your parade. By meandering, thinking and waiting, and hesitating, we turn an anthill of a circumstance into a pyramid of impossibility. Fighting this cowardice will condition and prepare you to do it again and again. You will always need to overcome it. Facing rejection young, early and often will propel you in the future to new places. Because in facing them, you will certainly gain some wins—some of which will change your trajectory in life and illuminate your light in a way never imaginable.

Law 54

Talk to people as if you have known them all your life.

Lesson 54: Familiarity eases the relations between us, humans. It is not our differences but our commonalities that bonds us in a way like no other species. We, all regardless of race, gender, histories, and preferences experience these same basic emotions: happiness love, sadness, anger, shame and appreciation. That is why it is especially important to shy away from condemning others. By broadcasting your misunderstandings and disregard for their cultures, preferences and perspective, you make the "other" person resentful of you and your differences. In terms of meeting those who you are not already acquainted, you must treat them with dignity and respect. Their position in life is not important, albeit a drunkard on the street or a monarch, your disposition should be the same. The authenticity in your speech and your extension of your hand should make them feel as if they grew up in the house next door to you. Be kind to those you meet along the way, for they may become your greatest allies.

Law 55

The people behind the scenes have names—learn their names

because they are just as important as those who are out front.

esson 55: This is elementary but it must be stressed: the importance of remembering a rson's name. In traversing life, you can do so with a bit more ease by keeping the mes of others in your front pocket. This law will serve you more than all others. The erage person does horribly in executing this; therefore, it presents an opportunity to our advantage. By saying a person's name you literally sound-off neurons that take him r her back to childhood. You make them feel more familiar to you and vice versa. You ould study the names of those who contribute to your light, especially. You should now the names of the people in the shops you buy things from. You should learn the ames of those who others always forget. Frequently, these people are the ones that ould be known the most. They tend to know the most. The stagehand's value to the lay is immeasurable. He may not get the glory that the actors do, but he certainly ontributes in a way that many actors cannot. There is always information in places and people like him. Learn their names and they will bind themselves to you. Their iendship to you will be like no other. The House of Illuminati has a long memory and s member should practice to this to perfection.

Law 56

Learn to control your impulses and emotions—be slow to anger.

Lesson 56: If the House is to remain strong, thriving through the centuries we must learn and teach our children that you must control your impulses and emotions, especially the emotion of anger. Anger is as natural emotion as any but it can get us into trouble and dangerous situations. Its combustibility can cause us to react in ways that our normal selves would never. You must keep in the forefront of your thinking the consequences of rash behavior. Rash behavior must be tamed and alternatives must always be considered. Gluttony also manifests itself in this way. Gluttony has been the downfall of many great kingdoms. The practice of overconsumption has led many of the greatest nations to find themselves in ruins. This practice first infects its leadership then trickles down to become the culture of its society at large. The desire for more and more, and to satisfy any insatiable urge is more dangerous than an enemy living in your home. Because at least you can kick your enemy out your home and get some distance between you and him. But when the enemy exists inside you—it is you—you are facing Goliath. You must build strength in the face of "yourself." You must discipline yourself. You must regularly practice denying yourself something that you love in order to train your mind, body and soul. If you are a gossiper, go a week without gossiping. If you love wine, go a period of time without it. If you eat lots of sugary foods, then go a month without. You must continuously challenge yourself. You must be disciplined in more ways than one to recreate yourself, control yourself, and be a better person. You must learn to manage your impulses and guide your emotional responses.

Law 57

Surround yourself only with those who are walking in the path of the light. Successful people don't hang around broke people.

Lesson 57: Eagles don't fly with ducks. Associate yourself with people who will support you along the path of light. Surround yourself with friends who are goal-oriented and going places as well. Your circle of friends should include people that you can learn from. Stay away from negative people and negative situations. Proverbs 13:20: Whoever walks with the wise becomes wise but the companion of fools will suffer harm.

Law 58

Provide no excuses, give an explanation only if required, but do offer an apology if the fault or error is found to be yours.

Lesson 58: Excuses are building blocks that have constructed pyramids of nothingness, castles of clouds and sound like fairy tales and fables. Learning the lesson after the test is not that helpful. If you commit a wrong, then you owe someone an apology. Provide a reasonable explanation when necessary to remedy doubts about your dependability.

Law 59

Men should always respect women for they are vessels in which the new light is created. When you seek a mate, find the highest quality vessel to bear the light.

Lesson 59: Frequently, the World's belief systems put women secondary to men. This is ludicrous. How can it be that the vessels that create the next generation and are cradles of the light are secondary to men? For the World knows that the creator of her is indeed like her. Men have for centuries intoxicated themselves with the belief that God is a man. In reality he is a she. Evidence of this is in the Bible where it states that "God is a jealous God" and "Her thoughts are not like your thoughts"—men cannot understand God, because man cannot understand woman. Therefore, women shall be regarded as goddesses. And goddesses are to be revered. We find these goddesses as our mothers, wives, sisters, and friends. It is not man's role to control her. Attempting to control any person, let alone a woman, is futile. It is not man's job to force her to cover herself because of his lust and his inability to control himself. She should determine her own attire. If she is in the light and respectful of herself and the laws, she will be tasteful in her clothing. In finding a mate with which to bare children, be wise and discerning. Be sure she is a person of high standing. If she is, she will do the same. Know that if you are living in your light actively and creatively, then you will attract a partner of the same caliber. You cannot get a racehorse out of a mule. Racehorses attract racehorses. Those with the light and living in their light will encounter others like themselves. Make no mistake about it.

Law 60

Beware of the watchers and keep a close eye on your enemies.

Lesson 60: The watchers you always have with you. Matter of fact, the watchers and th haters you always have with you. People are watching you and you probably don't ever realize it. People are clocking your every move including your enemies. Know wher they are so that you can avoid traps and ambushes.

Watchers must be handled with care. You must know that they are around while at th same time not noticing them. In fact sometimes you will not see them nor recogniz them. It is a delicate balance. On the one hand, if you become overly concerned with thei watching, staring and judging of you, it will cause you to falter in pursuing your light and your destiny. It will serve to only dim your light. On the other hand, to believe that n one pays attention to you, you are delusional. Everyone watches everyone. House members shall find that though we may become popular because of our gifts, ou connections and our ability to execute, we must find ways to retreat from the sights of the watchers. We must be leery of those that aim to expose the House. We must protect ou children from them as well. Often the watcher may double as your enemy. You mus keep them both close in mind, but remain far from them in distance. Only a fool believes there is no one that wishes ill upon him. The wickedness of man, the jealousies of the heart and the ruthlessness that is bestowed upon him because he is part beast causes him to be irrational and hateful. You have felt such emotions before. Knowing this you must understand that the most common of men has these same emotions inside him. Be wary of them—the watchers, but never be distracted by them.

Law 61

Accept the qualities of a person, even the bad ones, when they show you who they are.

Lesson 61:   Too often we suffer from this idea that we can make someone change. People can certainly change and they will, but our role in the change process is secondary to their own. Without a doubt, our light and love can cause a change in others but we must always allow people to be themselves. However, if you cannot accept who they are, then you must be willing to go separate ways. You should believe them when they tell you who they are and accept them. Yes, we have our moments when our behavior goes outside of normalcy, but if you spend enough time with a person it will certainly make itself obvious how this person is. Do not trick your instincts and the proofs that is a conduit to spending time with a person. If you believe this person is starved for attention and always seeking it, then perhaps you are right. If this individual is a selfish one, then surely you must have witnessed this selfish behavior on more than a few occasions. If this person is a giver, then without using the word "giver" you would not be able to describe her. First impressions have weight but be willing to let them go. Allow impressions to be gathered and seen over time, and you will certainly gain a better understanding of the person. Believe what you see and believe them to be the person that they tell you they are.

Law 62

Know more than one way home. Mix it up. Take different

paths/routes.

Lesson 62: Know your environment. Master the area in which you live. Do not always take the same route. It's okay to be a creature of habit but you have to take a different path every now and then. It will keep the watchers on their toes. Plus the more routes you learn to get where you are going, the better off you will be. Being flexible and adaptable will help you along the path to success. Taking different routes is like approaching a problem from a different angle—it teaches you to be creative.

Law 63

Use the light to make decisions—be decisive when the time

comes.

Lesson 63: Practice making decisions. Be decisive. The sign of a true leader is the ability to make decisions. Use the light and force within you to make the best decision. Apply the wisdom of the Laws and your learning to make a precise decision. Decide on the options with the most benefits and cause the least amount of damage.

Law 64

Tell no lies and do not share the secrets of others.

Lesson 64:   Do not tell a lie. Do not share the secrets of others. Always speak the truth
and speak truth to power whenever possible. Remember a man or woman is only as good
as their word, so mean what you say and say what you mean.

Law 65

ursue the calling of your light—chase your passion and live your

dreams for the Greater Light requires this.

esson 65: Your lesser light will not be at peace unless you pursue your passion. The
ursuit of money and getting rich is not a calling of the light. You build the treasury but
e treasury does not build you. Develop your gifts and talents, and money will be given
nto you. When you get money—divide it wisely and don't use it all once. Save some
or self and the maintenance of the light, save some for family, and save some for when
ou get old and the light begins to dim. Remember give some to the House. Run toward
our goal, chase after your dream until your heart is fulfilled. The only one who fails is
ne one who does not try. To learn that your dream is not what you want is not failure but
good try. Give it all you got, pray and thank God for the light within you.

Law 66

Keep these Laws, these Lessons, and your Commitments for there are consequences to breaking the Laws, the Lessons, and your Commitments. Write the Laws of Illuminati upon your heart. Live as if your life depended upon them. The path to success is guaranteed if you keep the Laws of Illuminati.

CHAPTER 2

A Letter to the Youth of this Present Age

Chapter 2

A Letter to the Youth of this Present Age

To the Youth of this Present Age:

O blessed and beloved Children of the Light, We, the Council of the Most Enlightened Ones of the House of Illuminati, charge you to commit yourselves to the path of success which is also the path of Light. We are grieved by the current state and condition which has befallen the youth of this present generation. So much so, that we break centuries of silence to write you a letter of hope dripping with the pains of our sorrow and lamentations. With so many youth around the world leaving systems of education as functional illiterates and so many others who aren't even allowed to attend school, we can only pray that this message will reach you and that you will have the ability to read it. This letter is all about how to be successful in this present age. Beloved, success is possible and success is obtainable by anyone who seeks it!

Everyone can be successful and we want to share with you the secrets of Illuminati which prior to now have only been shared with a chosen few. The House of Illuminati wants every youth to have the opportunity to be successful. But before we can share with you the secrets of success, we must share our lamentations and our pain with the youth of the present generation. For no success is possible without first some form of education. Therefore we seek to educate you as we deliver this gift because too much power too soon can be dangerous.

On one hand it seems as though the youth of this present age has lost their sense of purpose, lost their understanding of divine destiny, and lost their sense of self—ultimately losing the light within. On the other hand we are pleased with the hopeful spirit of

terminism that you have as evidenced by what we call the "Arabian Awakening" and
ers call the "Arab Spring." We are pleased with the collective force and spirit of the youth
ich rallied together to elect President Barack Obama, the 44th President of the United
tes of America. But before we praise you for things which we have found pleasing, allow
a few pages to speak on things which have caused us much concern.

Recently, the Council read a note believed to be from an American rap artist, Jay-Z,
sted on the Facebook social media website denouncing any affiliation with the House of
uminati. While this was quite insignificant to us, it was indicative of a growing and larger
oblem of which we have turned our attention. Immediately, we recognized the need to
dress the youth of this present age.

At first glance, we were slightly tickled, but upon insightful reading of the note from
y-Z, the Council of the Most Enlightened Ones became saddened as we reviewed its
ntents. In agreement with some of Mr. Carter's ("Jay-Z") statements, we will not critique
s letter but we will offer a few lines of commentary before moving on to the important
art of this appeal. Rhetorically, we ask, "How can one who has enjoyed the fruits of success
dhering to the Laws of Illuminati denounce participation?" One does not have to be an
fficial member of the House of Illuminati to be Illuminati. You only need to follow the path
f light and your light will automatically join in the energetic force of Illuminati. Yet for the
cord, Jay-Z, Kanye West, Beyonce, and no other American hip-hop artist are official
embers of the House of Illuminati at this time.

Illuminati is still pleased with them since they have exhibited a strong dedication to
e light within them and allowed their light to shine for the world to see. Every person that
as walked the face of the earth is a Child of the Light. But just to be certain, we decided to

check the official membership roll. A review of the roll of the House indicated that the la? American musician who was an official member of Illuminati was a 1925 Harlem-bor? singer, tap dancer, actor and musician. He made a significant contribution to the world nc only through his talented performances but through his political activism as well. He use the power of the light and his intellect to lend voice against the evil of racism an? discrimination in the American way of life. In a measure of his character, we are pleased t? see the artists, "Common" and "Queen Latifah" continuing along this path. We applau? "Common" as he speaks out for the cause of peace and we applaud "Latifah" for being ? powerful figure of positivity.

While we are clearing up a few rumors circulating out there among certain camps— do not be fooled by any false reports on how to become a member of the House o Illuminati. The House of Illuminati is a house of light and success. No one has ever had tc sell their soul to gain entry nor would we accept a member who would do such an act o? darkness. No member has ever had to injure a mother or any other family member tc become a part of Illuminati—do you realize how crazy and absurd that sounds to the Council of the Most Enlightened Ones. Any such claim that Kanye West sold his soul to? Illuminati and did harm to a member of his family so that he could be successful is false. We would not offer membership to anyone who would commit such harmful acts against the light! The Illuminati believes that one should honor their parents all of their days. Behaviors of darkness and evil are an abomination and should not ever be committed by anyone on the path of light and success. One's soul is not for sell and one's light should not ever be given away. The only deal that one must make to become a member of the House of Illuminati is the oath one swears to follow the Laws and the Commitments. This oath guarantees success. There is no secret conspiracy that the Illuminati would even take part hat would seek to hold one group back over another. The excuse of: "I am not successful cause I wouldn't sell my soul to Illuminati" is for lack of better words, some bullshit. Find entity other than the Illuminati to blame for your failure. The House of Illuminati wants eryone regardless of race, religion, creed, ethnicity, clan, sexuality, or ideology to be ccessful. The House of Illuminati does not discriminate when it comes to success. The re people that are successful, the more powerful the House of Illuminati becomes. Use ur Light-given talents and let no one stop you from being the best at whatever it is that u want to do with your life. And should you fail or feel that the odds are against you, call on the tenacious spirit of the Light to guide you and keep you on the path.

Once again, everyone can be a member of Illuminati, if they only agree to follow the th of the Light and to let the light within them shine for the world to see. Children, there a divine purpose and divine destiny inside each one of you. Your purpose is your calling hich you must fulfill in the service of good. The Light is good and does no evil. The Light eks to make the world a better place for all mankind. The Light is love and the Light ways seeks peace. At some point in your life and hopefully during the days when you are ung, you should commit yourself to the training of the your mind, the development of self, nd the responsible harnessing of your light and passion as you pursue your craft, whatever may be.

As watchers of history, we were there when Socrates was tried and executed for corrupting the youth;" we were there when Jesus of Nazareth preached a sermon telling all hose who congregated "that the Kingdom of Heaven belonged to those such" as the hildren; and we marveled as the children of Birmingham confronted an evil, racist system f government. The collective power of the youth has been known from the beginning of ime. If you strengthen the young, you can conquer. It's time that you, the children around the world, realize the collective power of your youth. Unite and conquer every issue that faces the world at this time! There is no challenge that is insurmountable—the Light will give you hope. There is no problem that cannot be addressed—the Light will give you voice. There is no obstacle, no government, no ideology too strong to be overcome—the Light will give you courage. The light inside of you must always be coupled with wisdom which brings us to our other lamentations.

The House of Illuminati grieves at the destructive forces which have set out on a path to rob the children of this generation and the world of its precious light. The youth of today do indeed perish due to a lack of knowledge. The issues of: violence and war, materialism, ignorance and anti-intellectualism, individualism, narcissism, the quest for money, the misinterpretation of respect, and racism are issues which affect the youth. These issues are pervasive worldwide and although they seem like adult problems, they are matters which start in one's youth and become diseases of the mind when old.

The level of youth violence in the world today is at an unprecedented and shameful high. Still addressing the American youth, and particularly the African American youth of Jay-Z's heritage (since Jay-Z felt it necessary to highlight your plight), Illuminati places a higher burden of responsibility on you because you live in a land where its citizenry has the freedom to think, the freedom to hold ideas and bring them into fruition, the freedom to speak one's mind, and the freedom to move about without any form of oppressive or governmental hindrance. It is your democratic privilege along with the Australian, Belgium, British, Canadian, French, Japanese, Mexican, and South African societies to think freely and be free. With all this freedom for opportunity and success, why do you feel it necessary to kill one another, glorify violence, make music about the use of drugs, and call your young women dogs, "hoes, and bitches"? Not only that, but you use the words of the colonial

pressors against one another as a badge of honor. The music says, "Nigga this and Nigga
t and bitch this and bitch that" every other word. You argue that by doing so you have
powered the word to powerlessness. Just so you know that doesn't make sense. White
ople would be crucified if they referred to a Black person as a "nigga" in this day and age
t African Americans expect that it is known worldwide that no one else can use the term
describe them. You are sadly mistaken. As the media carries your image 10,000 miles
ay to foreign places, cultural rules and in-group accepted behaviors do not translate. You
ust love yourselves first before you can expect anyone else to show you love. And if
meone treats you like you treat yourselves, they should not be blamed. It's time that the
rican American youth stepped up their game. The amount of gun violence in the African
merican community is unacceptable. Where is the voice of Jay-Z on this matter? Where is
e statement to the youth from Mr. Carter on this issue? If you wish to speak about the
oly Grail, use your voice and your light to address these matters; use your music to preach
ve and an end to the youth violence. The Council of the Most Enlightened Ones cannot
ear you Mr. Carter; therefore, we break our silence to bear your responsibility. Consider
is: in the entire nation of Japan, there were only 26 cases of violence involving a handgun,
hereas, there were over 400 gun-related murders in Chicago, an urban city in America,
one. There is a stark contrast between these two societies. There is no reason for the
outh to kill one another. It has to stop. The violence has to stop. You are brothers and
sters—all children of the light—and some of you act as if it's okay to kill someone for a
air of sneakers which cost $2 to manufacture in overseas sweatshops, or take a life
ecause of the colored dye in their bandanas, or because of which street a person happens
o live on. Who cares who wears red, blue, purple, or gold? What does the color of the dye
n the fabric have to do with the value of the light within a person? Is not a life worth more

than cotton and rubber spit from a tree? Those who commit these types of acts behave like the children of darkness—evil for no reason. You have no right to take the life of another human being. Were you there when the Light split darkness? Were you there when the Light created Day and Night? May the world always remember Emmett Till and may we never forget Trayvon Martin—two lives whose light was taken too soon.

We understand that some of the dark actions committed by the youth around the world are not your fault. There are no youth who own factories that make guns. There are no youth who own factories that make bullets. We understand that you are the products of your environment. We place the blame on your parents and their parents who were once upon a time youths but who forgot the lesson taught by one of the powerful members of the Illuminati—a Most Enlightened One of antiquity, King David. The Most Enlightened One King David said, "Remember your Creator in the days of your Youth." It's not your fault that some of your parents were not taught how to be good parents. It's not your fault that some of you are raising yourselves. It's not your fault that some of your fathers decided to abandon their responsibilities. No one got here on Earth by accident. Yet, there can be more love in some single-parent households than a home with four parents; but in the raising of a child, it's always good to have both mother and father. Some of these environmental circumstances can breed some terrible outcomes. But no matter how tough your life has been or how hard you think your struggle may be, there is no excuse for anyone to willfully take the life of another human being or be violent toward someone unnecessarily. This is wrong.

As we agree with Jay-Z's letter, it seems as though some African American youth have lost their identity and forgotten their history. Youth violence is one of saddest events that we witness. Have you lost the sense of pride for your people and your culture? Do you

t know the strength of the African Kings and Queens which spawned the richest and most
ucated dynasties? Do you not know of the North African academies which trained the
eeks in the sciences, mathematics, and medicine? Egyptian doctors were among the first
 document in papyrus books surgical methods and health treatments—and yes Egypt is a
rt of Africa. Let not the modern day Egyptian phenotype fool you into believing anything
her than this fact.

What does Cairo have to do with Chicago? Beloved children of the Light, we are all
om one source. How can you forget the Middle Passage and the Atlantic Slave Trade? Do
u realize how strong your ancestors were to have survived such a journey? If you think
e American form of chattel slavery was rough, then also consider the slave mines of Brazil
here the testicles of young men were castrated to stunt their growth in order to keep them
orking in the mines for longer periods of time. For the slaves to have grown into average
lult size or even experienced a growth spurt during normal adolescence would have
ndered them unable to enter the small passageways of the mines and become useless as
bor. The Brazilian slaveholders were brutally dehumanizing. There is no comparison of
ne form of slavery to another for it's all unconditionally inhumane and you end up
omparing one atrocity to another.   We know that the effects of these systems have
ndured long after their conclusion. A historical note as it relates to American slavery: the
mancipation Proclamation did not end slavery—it was no more than a wartime order to
ain more troops. Even with the adoption of the 13th Amendment of the U.S. Constitution
vhich formally abolished the institution of slavery and involuntary servitude in the U.S., the
mendment had a small loophole—"except as a punishment for crime"—which allowed
lavery to continue and flourish in certain parts of the South in a system called peonage
 and to some extent the crop-lien system also known as sharecropping). It wasn't until

December 12, 1941 that President Franklin D. Roosevelt signed circular No. 3591 whic

prosecuted Whites for peonage bringing that form of involuntary servitude (slavery) to a

end in the United States. Yet Black persons still continued to suffer in the highly racialize

society enduring the degradation and demeaning effects of racial segregation which we wil

talk more about later. During that period, Blacks would have to enter back doors of Whit

folk houses, ride in the back of public transportation, and work from sun up until sun dow

on someone else's plantation in order to survive.

Most importantly, the House of Illuminati recognizes that the youth didn't creat

this situation for themselves. This behavior is the product of hundreds of years of ethni

mistreatment. The **good news** is that the problem can be fixed and it can be solved in a da

if only the youth would unite and commit to the Laws of the Light and cease to trouble on

another ever again.

Stop the violence and commit yourself to peace, love, and neighborly actions. This

can be done in a day! Take your handguns and the bullets down to the local authorities. An

for those of the youth who say, "I cannot do such a thing because the gun has bodies o

blood on it," then take the gun and remove the bullets and bury them in a deep hole where

no other child will ever find it again. Jay-Z, why don't you put together a think tank of you

peers to get some of the guns out of the hands of the youth? Use some of your $5 million

treasury and create a gun buy-back/exchange program. But if the youth say, "I need my

piece in order to protect myself from someone else with a piece," then you have made the

case as to why all the youth must unite to form a worldwide truce and campaign against

violence. This can be done! Violence only begets more violence until you find yourself with

a war on your hand—a war that is already lost because if one child dies, the world suffers

from loss of light! Children unite worldwide in a voice against violence!

The Council knows that in places like Sierra Leone where you have boy soldiers engaged in civil war, it will be hard for them to unite against violence. In places like Iraq, Palestine, and North Korea, it will be hard for the youth to stand up against violence not because of the youth but because of the adults who train them and teach them do acts of darkness and evil. No child wakes up in the morning and says let me wage war against my fellow brother neither do they say let me go out and rape my sister. These are not natural acts of children and the ones who must be brought to justice are the adults who trained the innocent children to become terrorist monsters. As such in places like Iran, Iraq, or Pakistan, no child who believes in the teachings of the Holy Quran, wakes up and says let me strap a bomb on my back and blow people up. We have not found a single sutra in the Holy Quran which supports or condones such activity. We remember the glory of the Persian Empire in its antiquity and we recall the wars of the Persian Empire as well but not ever such violence aimed at an invisible ideology. The youth of this generation can change the world if they would cease to be violent but they must first be taught non-violence from the cradle and given an environment in which violence is neither accepted nor acted upon them. The adults of society must commit to such action.

Speaking to all of the youth around the world, materialism and consumerism are not callings and it pains the Council to see youth put more value into fashion, possessions, things and objects than they do the light within them. Back in the day, the Epicureans sought the finer things in life. Today this generation seeks "bling-bling." Your worth is not dependent upon how much you have in the bank nor by how much you are able to spend on some shoes, a video game, or a coat. You should not ever rob anyone or become a thief to obtain things. Your grandmother was right, "A liar and thief are bad people." Do not steal and do not lie to obtain material things. You do not have to chase the latest fashion trends or wear the highest costing name-brand labels in order to feel successful. You should s

your own standard and set your own trend. And just because you obtain those item

doesn't mean that you are successful either. For example you have a closet full of Nike an

Louis Vuitton, yet you live in your mother's basement without paying any rent—is tha

financially responsible behavior? You should not own a fancy car if you don't own th

carport that you park it under. There are people who live in places where they literall

walk on diamonds under their feet, and those diamonds have no value to them. If you mus

accumulate wealth, then acquire land and securities that can contribute to your survival an

that your children can also use one day. We are not arguing against having things of quality

but those things should not be so important that you lose sight of the real valuable things i

life. The Lessons of the Laws of Illuminati shall teach you these things. Obtaining profits i

never more important than the people that you serve. Remember that cotton is cotton—

whether Brand X stamps their name on them or there is no name on them at all, the same

cotton that grew in the field is used to make both pair.

Materialism and consumerism leads one on an unnecessary quest for money. There

is an ideology which suggests that you can get rich if you try and even the music of the

youth states, "get rich or die trying." But Beloved, the reality is that there is so much more

to life than money. There is so much more to life than treasures filled with riches and vaults

filled with gold. There is so much more to life than that and the sooner you realize this, the

better off in the long run and the quicker success and happiness will come. For it's not how

big your house is or how many cars are in the garage because ultimately none of these

things will matter. The Bible says, that the "love of money is the root of all evil." Last we

checked, material things were not needed on the other side. The Light needs none of it to

convene with the Creator. So live a life with meaning. Once again, it's okay to enjoy the finer ngs in life but your life should not be a quest for the finer things. If you agree with the

sician that said "get rich or dry trying," then you are already dead. Do not put your light

a path for something which it was not designed nor purposed for. There is no one born

Earth for which the purpose of their light was to just get money. Matter of fact, most

ildren of the light go over to the darkside because of a quest for money. Somewhere along

e way they were not taught the importance of human life, human relations, family and

ose things that make this experience on earth worthwhile. If all you got is your money,

en you don't have much. Get on the path to success and money will come to you. Become

ccessful and the riches will follow.

Beloved, education is the key to success. Seek as much knowledge and wisdom as

u can get. Ignorance and anti-intellectualism serves no one any good. Read all that you

n. Study all that you can. If the opportunity to go to school presents itself, go!!! Recently

Pakistan, a young girl Malala Yousafzai, was shot in the head because she wanted to go to

hool. In their culture, girls aren't allowed to be educated. Children of the world, everyone

iould be allowed to go to school no matter what gender they were born. No one had a

ioice in their gender and no one should be punished or treated differently based upon

eing a boy or a girl. You ought to want to be the smartest kid on Earth. Success requires

iat you know how to read and write and do math. If you can't read your work contract,

ien you will be cheated. If you cannot count your money, your boss will take advantage of

ou. If you cannot write, you will not be able fill out a job application. A right to an

ducation should be a universal basic fundamental human right for everyone on the Earth.

very system of government should seek to educate its young to be productive members of

ociety. If you want to be a rapper, learn the proper use of the language. If you want to be

n artist, learn mathematics so you know the right fractions to mix your paints. If you want to be a businessman, learn how to add so that you don't cheat others. Being educated is the coolest thing on Earth. There is no reason that you should need a calculator in order to figure out basic multiplication problems. Who benefits if you don't know how to read, write, or do math?—only those who would seek to have power over you. And the children of the light are too intelligent to fall victim to fools. The Illuminati reads and studies large volumes of information so that we can be knowledgeable on the progress of world events and two steps ahead of the children of darkness. You should seek to learn as much as you can. Success requires preparation and preparation requires that you study. Study requires that you read and read and read. Learn the difference between fact and opinion, between real and fake, and true and false. Commit yourself to education and instill this drive for education in your children. We must combat ignorance. The children of the world should unite and demand that they be educated!

Beloved children, individualism in the form of narcissism is not good. The philosophy of "me, myself, and I" benefits no one. Always seek to help others where possible. Helping others is a sign of greatness. You have a responsibility to look out for others, especially those who are younger than you and the very old. Life is not all about what you want. Sometimes you may be forced to make a decision that affects the greater good of others. You should not just look out for yourself but make sure that your family eats as well. If you have food, share it with your brothers and sisters. If you have more, then give. Give regard to the feelings of others. Be considerate of how your actions may affect others. Never fall victim to the "I got mine, you get yours," mentality. All the people on Earth are your neighbors. The people who live in France are neighbors with the people who live in China. The people who live in California are neighbors with the people who live in New Zealand. Look out for your neighbor for we are dependent on one another. Although

ne self-interest is healthy. You do have to make sure that you are taken care of just like
u have to make sure that you eat but you should seek equal treatment for those who
ke it to the dinner table. Everyone who sits at the dinner table should be able to eat.

There is a difference between individuality and authenticity, uniqueness, and
nuineness. You should celebrate your uniqueness and be authentic and real at all times.
u can only be second-best at being someone else. There is no one like you on Earth. The
ht within you is unique and belongs only to you. No one on Earth has the same light
mposition. Everyone is different in this regard. Be you—with your gold hair and a
ohawk if that's how you want to express yourself but always be respectful of others. Don't
vain and prideful in your beauty for there are more important blessings than your outer
pearance. Don't worry about how you look, the clothes you wear, or whether or not you
in with the "cool" kids. These image issues don't take away from the light within you. For
ample your ability to sing has nothing to do with the length of your hair. The gift of song
yours regardless of what your clothes look like. So regardless of how a person looks, or
en the color of their skin, you should respect them for their gifts, talents, and the light
ithin them.

Respect should always be given to people because there is light within others as
ell. The same light that makes you who you are is also within in others. Respect is often
isinterpreted and misunderstood. People have waged war and many fights have
appened because someone felt disrespected. Always be slow to anger and learn to control
our temper. Often times, it's a misunderstanding that can be cleared up with no problem.
espect is recognizing that another person has a right to be who they are and that as
nother human being or child of light, they have a right to exist on Earth just like you do.
hey have a right to live free, be free, and think freely just as you do. They don't have to

share the same religion, political idea, opinion or thoughts about an issue as you d▪

Respect is recognizing that a person has a right to make a decision for themselves an

understanding that they are free to do as they please so long as their actions do not harr▪

you or the greater good. Respect is accepting that people are different while treating ther▪

the same regardless of those differences. Respect is acknowledging the life and light tha▪

exists within someone else. Respect is accepting that others have a right to success and th▪

same resources on Earth just as much as you do. Respect is living together on this planet a▪

neighbors and allowing them to express themselves and be the best humans they can b▪

according to their own religion, sexuality, culture, philosophy, or society. Respect is no▪

infringing on the rights and happiness of others. Always be respectful of all persons anc

success will definitely follow! Children of the world, unite in a cause to be respectful of on▪

another and celebrate each other's differences and enjoy the things that you have ir

common.

Racism often results when persons lose respect for others based upon the race

ethnicity, or skin color of a person. And when the respect is lost, one group feels more▪

superior to the other and begins to treat them differently simply because of the color of

their skin or ethnic group. The more powerful group will ultimately control the resources▪

and lives of the less powerful racial group. Once this happens, racist actions have occurred.

If you think or believe that you are better than a person or group of persons because of skin

color differences, then you are a racist. Racism is wrong because it is disrespectful to the

life and light within another person. You should always treat people equally no matter what

their color may be or what ethnic or religious group they belong. Remember we must

celebrate our differences and enjoy the commonalities. Deep on the inside we are all the

same. Racism is evil because it destroys the mind of all involved. Those who have the

wer become oppressive and those who are treated unfairly become psychologically
ttered. The mind of the minority group becomes so battered that it destroys their
nking to the point that they believe more so in what they can't do than what can do. So it
comes impossible for them to believe that a Jay-Z could become successful on his own
rd work and merit. The system becomes the enemy and a belief is formed that somehow
e system will work against them just because of their skin color. White folk around the
orld have to realize the part they have played in creating these social evils. American
hites and British Anglos and the even Germans must accept their role in the way
cialized societies are the way they are today. Minorities still suffer because of the years of
eatment due to racism which has destroyed family units and communities. Tell us where
e Native American is today? Tell us where the Australian Aborigine is today? Tell us
here the Zulu is today? They are in a condition of dire straits in some cases due to racism.
ffirmative action and access to educational opportunities should be allowed until equity of
sources can be guaranteed by every government on Earth. Racism is pure ignorance. We
dvise minority groups to guard their image in their media and their music. Guard the
nage that the world sees of you. If the people of Bali only see a certain group characterized
s pimps, thugs, and gangsters in the movies and music, then they will only believe the
nages that they see. Create positive self-images among your youth and eliminate the
egative images which seem to have taken hold. In order for racism to end today, it must
tart with the youth of today. For racism takes time to work itself out of a society—consider
ne Afro Peruvian pallbearers of Peru, who to this very day are placing the dead in graves
ecause of some old racial baggage from the 1800s. The youth of today must make a
ommitment to end racism and to teach their children respect for different cultures. The

Light does not know color! Success does not know color! Anyone can be successfu' Children of the world, unite to end racism!

Throughout this letter it may have seemed as though the Council has paid attentio to and highlighted the causes of the African American youth. In a way we have becaus African American youth should be an example to the world as to what can be achieved wit determination above insurmountable odds. The tenacious spirit of the African America people and culture throughout time bears great witness to the survival strength of th human race. Their story and their success is one of great hope and many lessons can b learned by all citizens of the world. It was the African American children who marched protested, and demonstrated to secure their right to participate in a society free of racia discrimination. And they were successful!! Take note from their struggle, learn their techniques, and adopt their strategies to achieve freedom and harmony in your society. Learn about Shirley Chisholm, Dr. Martin Luther King, Jr., Nelson Mandela, Malcolm X Barbara Jordan, Medger Evers, and Mahatma Ghandi and so many others who struggled for the causes of education, justice, non-violence, and peace.

The Council has also been seemingly critical in its analysis of the youth of the present age and we have. But we are also equally pleased and hopeful that the youth of this generation will rise up and be the best citizens of the world that history has ever seen. You have so much knowledge at your fingertips--use it to your advantage! We were pleased to see the youth of Egypt and Turkey begin to demand a change. The age of dictatorships and theocracies should be over. These forms of government have only served to amass power and wealth in the hands of a few. There is nothing wrong with living under divine law but people should have a right to enjoy their lives freely under whatever system of governance they so choose. The reality is most nations are free—democratic in some form or another:

stralia, Belgium, Britain/UK, Canada, Europe, France, India, Japan, Mexico, New Zealand. st nations are free and democratic. The few that aren't just happen to contain over a lion people including China and the Middle East. It's time for oppression to end. There is reason why the Jews and Palestinians can't be friends—they are blood-related scendants of two brothers. There is no reason why women can't drive in Saudi Arabia d little girls are kept out of school. Everyone should have a right to enjoy life as freely as manly possible. So we are always pleased when the collective spirit of the youth comes gether for good. Learn new ways to do old things.

Remember Socrates who was charged, convicted, and executed for corrupting the inds of the youth. Well, Socrates was actually guilty. But how could such a free society at supported philosophical thought come to such a conclusion. Be not fooled by Plato's count and defense of Socrates because as his student, Plato did a great job at telling the ory of his teacher. However, Socrates taught a student by the name of Critias who became e leader of Athens. During his short time as leader, Critias killed thousands of Athenians, ole a vast amount of their property, and sent many into exile and hiding. Socrates ntinued to enjoy his freedom during this time and didn't speak a single word of protest gainst Critias for his actions against the people. Socrates educated a mass murderer and d nothing to help his people. Now to Socrates' defense, Critias had a mind of his own. ritias is responsible for his own actions. But the silence of Socrates while such evils were ommitted was hard to forgive by his jury; therefore, they sent him to his death. Beloved, ways err on the side of right. The problem is in knowing which side is right. To figure that ut, you must be educated—learn all that you can and always do good! It's okay to dream! t's okay to aspire to greatness! We all should set out on this path. And the first step should e toward the schoolhouse.

One of the Most Enlightened Ones of antiquity, King David, said, "Remember your Creator in the days of your youth." This is sound and wise advice that should not be taken lightly. Seek to know the Light and in the process you will come to know yourself. This will also build character and help you come to respect others, not for what they do or who they are but for no other reason than the same light within you is the same light within them. It a basic reverence for the Light which ought to lead to respect. It is our hope that one day every person in the world could taste the freedom of democracy. It is our hope that ever child will one day be able to think creatively and freely and engage in ideas that lead to better and safer world. Imagine the limits of knowledge if everyone were taught a basi education which allowed them to read and write. The future of the human race depends on this. The success of the human race depends on this. To that end, children of this present generation, beloved of this present age, unite worldwide on the path to success which is also the path of light! Success is obtainable for everyone! Love everyone!

And now we close in love with a poem written by Dr. Benjamin Elijah Mays, "Life i Just a Minute":

Life is just a minute—only sixty seconds in it.

Forced upon you—can't refuse it.

Didn't seek it—didn't choose it.

But it's up to you to use it.

You must suffer if you lose it.

Give an account if you abuse it.

Just a tiny, little minute,

But eternity is in it!

lk in the Light!

minati, Signed and sealed in the Year of the Light 2013

;.—A Message to the Old Ones

Also, the Council would like to speak a word to the adults who may read this letter
the youth: We must create a world in which the youth can grow, learn, and live safely and
ely. For after all, the youth will one day run the world; therefore, we have an obligation
teach them in the matters and affairs that will guarantee continued success of the Earth.
agine the peace that can exist, if we teach them peace. Imagine the love that can exist, if
e teach them how to love. Imagine the amount of greatness and success that can exist, if
e teach them the responsibility of service to others. The time is now for all of us to make
is commitment. We should end all wars now including the ones developing in Syria and
gypt. America, Britain, and any other civil nation should not initiate a single military
tion against the nation of Syria until the people of Syria unite against the internal system
hich has waged annihilation using chemical weapons of destruction against them. And it
only then—when the people of Syria have banded their light collectively against the evil
d darkness that prevails within their borders, then foreign nations should come to the
ssistance of the people. The people of Syria must take action first. If the populace will
peak out against the atrocities and ask for help, then any nation with a compassionate
oncern can act diplomatically on their behalf. The words of Martin Luther King, Jr.,
njustice anywhere is a threat to justice everywhere," ring truth in this situation. And
hould the populace speak collectively, the world may not need to assist the Syrians in
oing what they can do for themselves.

Toward this end, all wars must cease immediately and we must pursue the causes of peace to ensure the future of us all. This note also goes out to the people of Turkey. The youth of Turkey should band together with a collective spirit to ensure a progressive future fueled with success. It would be wise for the Turkish Republic to strengthen its young by educating and training them in all aspects of every craft. The power to define and the power to participate in one's own destiny are critical to the self-actualization of the individual. Neither should China and Korea (hopefully the Koreas unify soon) seek to control the minds of its people. Free democratic processes and freedom to think are the basic fundamentals of human rights. Additionally, Japan should clean up its nuclear program and Iran should abandon its desire to obtain one. Alternative forms of energy are available which can sustain nations without the use of nuclear mechanisms. We have a duty to unite around the world in the name of peace! Every nation should be committed to the goal of peace!

Chapter 3

The House of Illuminati

CHAPTER 3

THE HOUSE OF ILLUMINATI

To all those who wish to know the secrets of the Light, contained herein is the history of The House of Illuminati. The House of Illuminati is an ancient order of the Egyptian Dynasty of Ra. It died but was revived following the years of Christ as the learned soldiers of the faith set out to tell anyone who would listen about the power of the Light. Following a series of persecutions, those who knew the power of the Light were forced into an underground existence and way of life or faced death at the hands of those who feared the Illuminati. It was at this point, somewhere around the third century A.D., that the House of Illuminati became a society of secret members. Those who would become members of this secret society were sworn defenders and protectors of the Light, known to each other by hidden signs and the ancient symbol of the Eye of Horus. The Eye of Horus had come to symbolize the power of the Light and its knowledge in both this life and the next. And with this, the House of Illuminati was reborn.

The story of Creation and the Illuminati Creed attests to: "In the beginning of the universe, the Light shined and split darkness. In the beginning of the universe, the Light moved and made the heavens and the earth and everything thereon. In the beginning, the Light became a part of everything it had created. The Light still exists within all of us and all its creation inherits the Light from generation to generation." It is this Light and the secrets of its manifestation and possession, which the members of the House of Illuminati guard unto death. For all those who understand the knowledge and wisdom of the Light and how to use its gifts will be successful in the fulfillment of all their dreams and desires. The Laws, ssons, and Commitments govern how to apply and use the gifts of the Light. Success is aranteed for all those who enter the House of Illuminati.

Its members were like a family—a house that included the most esteemed and elite the community. Among its ranks were philosophers, business leaders, doctors, scribes, tists, musicians—the most respected and the most powerful. Admission to this House was ined only through the commitment to the Laws and the teachings of their Lessons. Those no swore to follow the path of Light, swore with their life to defend and protect the owledge of the Light.

Yet as with every house, division can enter forming factions and groups. The House Illuminati differed over the direction and expansion of the 7 Commitments of the uminati. One group believed that the Laws of the Illuminati should remain the same day, and forever, since antiquity. While others in the House of Illuminati believed that the ws, the practices and beliefs should evolve with the historical times. As a result those who lt that the Laws should remain static over time formed a group which we called the ddfellows. Until this day, the Oddfellows remain in darkness about the issue. Those who elieve the Book of Illuminati, the laws of the Illuminati, grows with the times remain the ue House of Illuminati. The Laws reference philosophical opinions, include a variety of ssons and examples, and credits individuals who have contributed to the Illuminati hilosophy. As some of the laws will sound familiar, you will note that the same Light of the luminati is the same light that inspired the scriptures of the Bible, principles of the Quran, eachings of Buddha, just to name a few... The Laws of Illuminati continually write hemselves and may change based upon new revelations of the Light. They will and forever ontinuously live and breathe but their number shall always be sixty-six. There are sixty-six aws of the Illuminati.

For the last thousand years, the House of Illuminati has existed in secret in every society known to man where civilized behavior governs the action of peace. In the American society, however, the House of Illuminati has been confused with a quest for money, power, and respect. It has come to symbolize a secret society among entertainers and celebrities alike. This incorrect representation makes it appear as though the members of the House of Illuminati are concerned only with fame, fortune, and status. This could not be farther from the truth. The House of Illuminati grieves at this idea for although its members were once the most highly regarded and richest of leaders, its mission was never fueled by the pursuit of money or the want of "Benjamins," "scrilla," "paper," "cheese," "cheddar," "ducats," "dineros," or "dollars." The House of Illuminati, although a rich house has not ever concerned itself with the trivialities of the treasury except to conduct the business of the Light. The House of Illuminati is all about letting your light shine and being true to the gifts and talents within you. When you are true to your calling and your passions, riches shall always follow you. Your gifts will make room for you. Do your job so well that the world will recognize you for the service that you have done—sing your songs, paint your paintings, craft your crafts—show vast amounts of love, and respect will be given unto you. Once you have developed yourself and trained your mind to its highest potential, power will come without effort for men will request that you lead them. You do not have to sell your soul in order to be successful. Matter of fact, the most successful people are those who would not sell their soul, those who would not sell their talent on the market, and those who stayed genuine to who they were as a person. The moment that you are willing to compromise yourself to get wherever you think you want to go in life, you are already dead. We are not suggesting that one should not comprise or make deals to get to the top, for this always has to happen in some form or another. We are arguing against compromising your aracter and constitution as a human just to score big. This is not tolerated in the House of minati nor does the House of Illuminati ever make a deal which forfeits the soul and light a person. The notion that you have to kill to gain membership is false and has not ever en the case. We are sworn defenders of the light and to destroy light would cause hurt to e Greater Light. Be neither seduced nor convinced that taking life or destroying light is mething that must be done. The act of doing such things is purely of the darkness and is nsidered evil by the House of Illuminati—something that we would have no parts. Along e way, other myths and rumors will be made clear. Clarity is usually provided in the ssons associated with each Law.

The House of Illuminati wants every person on earth to be prosperous, wealthy, rich ot necessarily financial but spiritually and mentally), free, and happy. And this can be hieved if the world would follow the path of the Light. The amount of love on the path of e Light can change the world. Love is a powerful, energetic force. It is the product of the ght—and when two light sources meet, the amount of energy increases. Self-actualization possible and so is success! There are levels to this House and self-actualization is near the p. Once you reach this level, you will not only come to know yourself and others but also our Creator. At the highest level, you will truly know the Light and walk with the light. At e highest level, your light will always shine—your mere presence will be electrifying and nergetic. Just let the world see and feel the light within you!

Contained herein are the Laws of the House of Illuminati. They are secret only to hose who do not know the Light and made known to all those who seek to know. The Laws xist to guide and govern those who are walking on the path of light on their way to success. he Rituals including the Illuminati Prayer, Illuminati Creed, and the Signs of the Illuminati re provided as well so that the true members can be known.

CHAPTER 4

The Rituals

Chapter 4

The Rituals

Contained herein are the rituals which govern the order of the House of Illuminat

Recorded are the procedures for new entrants, orientation, and protocol for the use of th

Illuminati Prayer, the Illuminati Creed, the hidden signs, and general conduct of Hous

business.

The leader of a House of Illuminati is called "The Most Enlightened One" and thi

person should preside from the eastern side of the room. The Most Enlightened One i

assisted by two house leaders: the Senior Guardian and the Junior Guardian. The chaplair

is called "The Lightkeeper" and is responsible for the prayer.

Although anyone can follow the Laws of the House of Illuminati and be successful

those who wish to become official members must be introduced to the House by one who is

already a member. After an extensive interview, the new entrant shall be called to the

House for an initiation ceremony. New entrants on the first level of knowledge and the first

Commitment shall be called Lamp Lighters.

The detailed initiation ceremony is not ever written but once and that is when a new

House is formed. A written copy of the ceremony in cryptic form shall be placed in the desk

of The Most Enlightened One. The desk is called the "Light House" and is ceremonially

guarded by the Senior and Junior Guardian. Under penalty of breaking our Commitment,

the ceremony shall remain a hidden mystery of the House. There is some business of every

house that should not be published for the streets (didn't someone in your family ever tell

...u that). At each level of the House, new entrants must study the Laws, Lessons, and ...mmitments appropriate for the knowledge for which they will receive.

There are certain signs and grips by which you shall know and recognize a member ... the House of Illuminati and by which members recognize each other. New entrants shall ...arn a handshake, a secret word, and a sign to correspond to their level in the House. The ...st word that the Lamp Lighters will learn is: Lux. And when asked by other members to ...part the word, it shall be given in reverse order: X-U-L. The second word that new ...trants will learn after their final Commitment is: Fiat. And when asked by other members ... impart the word, it too shall be given in the reverse: T-A-I-F. The word which is given ...so lets other members in the House know at which level of light one has achieved. The ...ords "LUX FIAT" are Latin for "Let there be light". The handshake and signs will be ...ustrated below.

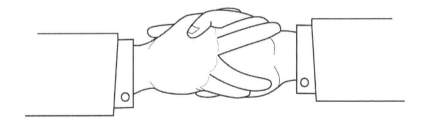

The handshake is a traditional handgrip with the first two fingers extended touching the wrist of your brother or sister. This grip must be done in the most secretive way such that no passerby knows that the grip has been exchanged.

Another visible sign of Illuminati members is the wearing of a gold-faced watch with a diamond on the six; and the number six is not enumerated but represented only by the gem. The Most Enlightened one shall where a silver or white gold chain with the Eye of Horus and a sun affixed in its center. If a ring is worn it shall also have the Eye of Horus in onyx inlayed on a golden ring and a diamond for the center of the eye. Golden Illuminati pocket watches are often worn by the highest ranking members. The Eye of Horus is embossed on the inside of the cover on the watch. Like the watches worn on the wrist, there is a diamond gem for the six.

Members of the House of Illuminati take great care of their temple—the body; for the body is the house of light. Physical exercise and a nutritious diet are hallmarks of a good Illuminati member. Smoking and imbibing substances which alter the mind ultimately will destroy the temple. Cleanse your temple from these negative products because they will serve only to destroy your light. Take time to grow and eat the purest of foods. You should eat fruits and vegetables from the earth daily. Avoid food laden with unnatural ingredients.

ke care of your heart and your mind. Proper care of the body must be taken to enjoy a

ng and prosperous life.

These rituals have been handed down for centuries. The House of Illuminati will

om time to time convene to adopt and modify its code according to the present age.

CHAPTER 5

THE ILLUMINATI CREED

Chapter 5

The Illuminati Creed

We believe the Light, "the Greatest Light," is the Creator of the Universe.
There is no power higher or greater than that of the Light.
We believe in the beginning, the Light shined and split darkness.
We believe in the beginning, the Light moved and made the heavens and the earth and everything thereon it.
The Light was and will always be from beginning to end.
And should the Light cease to be, there will be no more.

A part of the Greatest Light is in all living things.
The Lesser Light is the part of Greatest Light in all living things and is inherited from generation to generation but uniquely bestowed upon each individual.
The Lesser Light is a gift to creation from the Greatest Light.
Each of us must use the Lesser Light according to the Greatest Light's purpose and will for us.

We believe we must use the Light given to us for good and not evil.
We believe if we use the Light according to its purpose, treasures shall be added unto us.
We believe that each person must let their light shine or suffer and lose it.
We believe that it pleases the Greatest Light when we let our inner light shine.
We believe that money, power, nor respect should ever be sought but are gifts of the Lessor Light through hard work, determination, and education.
We believe that no one should prostitute their light and sell their soul for its use because all things are possible for the one who lets his light shine.
We also believe that all those who experience the power of the Light, experience love. And those who do not know the Light, do not know love.

We believe the House of Illuminati is the most sacred house of the sworn defenders of the Light.
We believe that the House of Illuminati is the keeper of the mysteries of the light and all who shall enter this House are bound to its Laws, Lessons, and Commitments.
We believe that the Laws of the House of Illuminati will always lead to success.

We believe that we must protect the light within the temple provided for us.
And when that light no longer shines within us, we are no more;
And the Lesser Light shall return to the Greatest Light.

CHAPTER 6

The Illuminati Prayer

Chapter 6

The Illuminati Prayer

(To be spoken by the Lightkeeper at every initiation ceremony and each member of Illuminati shall be taught a passage as they progress through the levels of light.)

rd, make me an instrument of your light,
here there is darkness, let me be light;
here there is there a void, fill it;
here there is suffering, relief;
here there is opportunity, obtain it;
here there are insurmountable odds, hope;
here obstacles seem to prevail, determination.

Master of Light,
ant that I may not so much seek to be inspired, as to inspire;
be blessed, as to be a blessing;
be known, as to know.
be loved, as to love.

I

or it is in shining bright, that darkness is overcome.
is in uplifting others that we are uplifted,
nd it is in being the greatest person that I can be that I share in the Greatest Light.
nd along the way, may I never be tempted to sell my light and lose my soul.

J

ay the light you have placed within us shine.
ord, let that light shine for the world to see.
rant us the courage to use the light according to thy will and purpose,
rant us the strength to endure the pain along the way;
nd give us the knowledge to know when to shine and when to glow.
ay we never make you ashamed of us in the pursuit of the path which the light has shone.
ay we always be true to its purpose and its calling using the light for good and not evil.

low Lord, give us a light to see our way through the darkness.
Ve thank you for the light of creation.
Ve thank you for the light that you have placed within us.

"I

nd when my temple that holds the light begins to crumble,
rop it up on every leaning side.
nd when my eye grows dim,

Continue to be a light upon my path even unto my grave.
May my light always serve the Greater Light.
To your glory and honor.
Amen.

HE LIGHT PLAN: YOUR PERSONAL PLAN FOR SUCCESS

WRITE YOUR VISION, GOALS, AND PLAN FOR WHAT YOU WANT TO DO IN LIFE. BE VERY SPECIFIC ABOUT HOW YOU INTEND TO GET TO YOUR DESTINATION.

THE ILLUMINATI BUSINESS PLAN

If it wills you to meet success financially, then choose four of your most trusted and closest friends and join in an agreement to be wealthy with one another.

4 MOST TRUSTED AND CLOSEST FRIENDS:

1._____   2._____

3._____   4._____

Choose these folk wisely, for friends and money do not often mix. Each person of your Illuminati team should save individually for one year. After the one year of savings, pool your savings together and utilize the total toward the down payment on the purchase of an investment property, rental property, or a business. If your neighborhood does not have grocery store, buy one. Create ideas that will generate you income for the rest of your days. If you can do this and execute it, you will have bound yourself to success for lives to come. You will not only bring about success for you, but success for your children and theirs.

Made in the USA
Middletown, DE
24 June 2020